CW00867987

1

By

Ed Chandler

This book is dedicated to all the writers.

4

Contents:

Preface

Only is there a post face?

Now I should warn you that this book is not like anything else on the shelf. It's not my "Run Of The Mill" either, and is in no way connected to the "Run Of The Mill" series. Instead this book is simply going to be 'Drivel'. That is to say it's a collection of unusual things, little one-liners and odd shades of poetry that will in some small way I hope inspire other writers in years, months and days to come.

There will be questions to which no one might have an answer, not even me. We'll go into film a bit and those moments that you know are the product of Hollywood, for instance the jungle noises you often here in such "Tarzan" or similar epics, well, despite having not been on safari myself, I do know that some of the noises were more manmade than having actually come from the animals themselves.

But technology and time moves on and films grow, some of them, the ones that are true to life, will get as close to reality as they can, if not closer.

Going back on myself a moment and I might do it again later...

Preface as opposed to post face, because preface is the foreword, it's at the beginning, which is the start of this 'Drivel' and then I thought, could you have an opposite to the preface and call it post face, for the opposite of 'forward' is backward, but not sideways, or is it?

Now there is an interesting observation, for forwards, that is to move ahead, or in the direction that you face, could well be the preamble route that is an introduction to the opening of the story. So forward and preface go together thus. But in terms of direction we are talking a different kind of foreword, and any writer has to enjoy that, the fact that there are two words there, both sounding the same, but spelt differently. And there are others, for the whole 'Where' and 'were' business, not to mention 'there', 'their' and 'they're', has its own complications.

We're all taught in school this grammar business, but to a writer, to use the incorrect word, might actually be better than using the correct word, just as the human mind when reading something, it will only take in the first few letters and often more than not you can actually put some of the letters in the wrong order, just as long as the first letter and last letter of the word are correct.

I think that's right, I'm not going to try it. I might use the wrong word, perhaps say write, when I mean right, are forward and not foreword. Well anyway preludes and postscripts aside, let us move on swiftly and begin.

Inside...

I find that if you want to write anything then start at the noisy end of the cafe, or in a busy bar, anywhere you can overhear conversations, but won't really stand out to much, being inside is always best.

Make the most of going to a writers or poetry group, even if you've never written anything, but want to. Firstly there the poetry groups where people read their own poems and others will give feedback, which is good, but what you want to do is be the one taking the odd note or two, pinching the odd line of text from a random poem...

It's not really stealing the idea, it's more listening and being able to find your own voice, but by being able to listen, I find you can then write a whole lot better.

It's why I started this book...

Of course it helps if you want to actually write something. And there are lots of great books about creative writing, or how to write poetry, how to sell it and how to get it published, all of which are great. Of course there is self-publish now and it's taking the book world by storm almost, as why go to all the bother of having to get an agent and then send of proofs, and edit and re-edit, choose covers, decide on costs and all that, yes there will be many a hill to climb, but think of the view from the top, the rewards also should be good if you get it right.

Only there isn't always a right, and you might find that some books will waffle on about a "Target Market", who the book is for and all that, but actually you might only want to write it for you, your friend, your mum, or a loved one.

You might like me have a collection of really random and odd things and just bung them altogether and call it a book, for why not, what's in a book anyway, does it really need to have a plot and all that?

For yes there are the "genres" and the many themes of writing, a poem is not a play, but you can have poetry within a play. Writing for stage and screen are separate, but in some ways they will have similarities, just as a murder mystery can be a murder mystery in play, prose, short story, on screen or in a short poem.

They took a gun,
They fired a shot,
They were dead,
And that was that.

They say that we all have a story, and if that's where you're going to start in writing, then fine, but who is the story for? Is it because you feel you have a good story that would make a book? Or is it that now at this point in your life, you've always wanted to write a book and here it is no matter what the subject.

As there is a mass of subjects that one can write about, with or without knowledge on the subject matter, I could write a book about the dynamics of physics and the properties of combined chemical reactions in the brain, the human anatomy from the patient's point of view.

What I write is personnel to me, but in some way reflects on what's inside us all, for most of the so called target audience will be familiar with a murder mystery, there will be those who enjoy reading poetry, including the old romantics, Hemmingway, or selected poems by Steve Cawte.

Whatever you write, you hope that if you get published either by going through an agent and then publishing company, or if you just self-publish and use a print on demand service, I hope that when the book comes out and you get a copy, and you hold it, smell it and read it, look back over those words you typed onto the computer, your words.

Whole sentences and paragraphs, or lines of poems, maybe conversations as one character goes to other and strikes them in a carefully written stage direction.

I say to you then, please let me know, for I might like to read your book, and I'm sure you'll find others that will want to say "Well done" and ask if they too can read it?

Now back tracking to forwards and forewords, when it comes to words like that I suddenly remembered that a 'Potato Waffle' has the same spelling for just the word 'waffle' itself, and I'm sure there are others, but sadly I don't recollect them off hand, or should that be remember them at this point?

Either way it's no matter, just that to have the wrong word might not be 'write', but more wrong. But in some way slightly amusing, not to make humour of the mistake, but to make humour in the context. For context is more relevant in using the word, for the way you use the word, gives it the meaning to which you prefer.

As a writer myself I tend to rely on the technology at hand, I trust a machine to give me the correct spelling, or if I misuse some form of Grammar, or when in a rush I type "form" and not "from", I hope the machine picks it out.

Inside then is a great place to be for it's warm in here mostly, but when the sun is out, and the weather is good and the beaches are packed, the queue for an ice cream is long, but then as it gets a little cold and the sun starts to set, and if you are a child and mum cries out "Come inside at once", and you do...

Back inside, in the home, it's where the heart is or something like that, but it also denotes to a more sinister place, in some small way of inside, the inside of a prison cell for instance. So you see the word inside can itself conjure up a wide range of different meanings.

For we have feelings inside of us, thoughts, guilty pleasures, perhaps even desires. Some keep secrets inside, some are inside themselves, never venturing beyond the comfort of their own little world, and the world itself. Earth, the planet we inhabit it's inside a vast Galaxy, there are other planets besides this one and other galaxies far off beyond the view of my eyes.

I often smile, but inside my sorrow shows, there is a glow around me, but I could be dark inside.

Inside the train of thought the travellers watched the scenery pass them by, some were on mobile phones, some listened to music, some put pen to paper, but all just let the scenery pass them by.

As the momentum of my insides stopped, I knew that all was not well.

Inside this story the real meaning is the man who is not all he seems.

'A medium sized man with glasses sat next to a beautiful blond in a cafe, he picked up a newspaper and glanced at it. He was fidgeting, he had a look of intelligence about him, and as he put down the paper to look at his watch, he noticed the time was exactly three o'clock in the afternoon. The man who was as plain as any other man, could have easily hidden more. Across from him the young lady took out a cigarette and then man obliged her with a light. As he took out the lighter from his pocket a solitary Lego brick fell to the floor.'

Inside a cafe the other day I noticed Shakespeare, Noel Coward, and Ian Fleming all sat at the same table.

This is my idiosyncrasy, it's what's inside that counts.

Now to me we all have the same insides. That is a heart, lungs, kidneys, a large and small intestine. Nerves or a nervous system, which does not mean that it's 'nervous' as in afraid, worried or edgy, these are just forms of 'nerves'.

Some would say that there is a soul, but I disagree with this, as although the soul is not a physical object like the heart, it is however the person as a whole, for the soul is more about the person you are, how you react to things, what you feel, what you say, and in some small way what you write, it comes from inside, it is made within you.

Come rain or shine, but better for clear and cool summer days. Moving around in the snow is slower than taking a short walk in sandals down a beach. I'm more pleased when the weather is good, I feel good. I can get out and go places, see and do things. I can go out in the rain, but I often have to go in the car, and should snow fall, it's always best not to go too far. But come rain or shine the weather makes me realise it's not that much of a problem to go out at all!

So if I'm inside or outside writing, I can always find at least one thing to 'right' about, or at least I hope I can.

For inside we fear the writer's block, but I actually embraced my writers block, wrote about it and overcame it by looking for things to write about, looking at writing exercises, doing things, going places, sitting inside and looking back over the odd line I had written down, making sense of an old poem that is not yet in with any of the Poetry books I have written.

Inside the writers stare there is a glare of the human within. For do you have a writers stare, can you glance across a room and see the words falling all around you, picking up shreds of information and conversation.

For to see and listen, rather than talk, for we all have two ears and only one mouth, so listen twice as much and type twice as much for you should have two hands, eight fingers and two thumbs...

If anyone has ten fingers, I'd like to know where there two thumbs are, or have they suddenly grown an extra finger on each hand, or perhaps two on one.

When we are inside we are closed from the outside, we can be alone, away from prying eyes. Many pleasures can be sought and ought one not to mention the art of love, but simply partake of naked wine and divine to one's desire.

Sit and watch a film perhaps, with popcorn and feel good inside as you look back to the bleak world and say goodbye.

Inevitably we'll end up inside a wooden box, the coffin to which we lay in, the last place to be inside as death begins but never ends.

Inside I'm thinking it's time to change, cheer up and reflect on what's inside this book.

Is it relative, does it serve purpose? Hold on, those are questions and should come at that chapter and that chapter alone.

For what is a question doing inside the inside?

Well its part of the drivel that makes this book up, the little one-liners and the odd random section of poetry, the going on of films and stuffing it all together to get an end result.

I imagine being inside, I watch a show, the spotlight is like sun gleaming onto the stage.

So my dear reader I apologise in advance, for the drivel that shall follow and forever by apart of the pages that make up this book.

If Fleming, Hemmingway and Dickens were all inside, locked forever in a jail, cast off as if swine, but in time they write and the poetry, the stories, the adventures, they all become all too real, and the feel for pleasure, the need for speed and the aspect of danger can be found all on one page.

We are at the opening game, it's not inside, for some games are played on fields, some between sheets, some at a desk, and some games are played as part of a team are all alone.

Inside this great blank verse, you might find a nugget of wisdom.

We're inside my mind, and it's not as vast as it appears, it's open and full of useless bits of information, but every now and then one little item pops out, a nugget of pure intellect. Often more than not it's that little word, those few little things, the bits of randomness that you pick up as a writer that will eventually lead to something more.

Watching Herons nest, or Peregrines fly, going out and talking to others, being part of nature on an RSPB reserve, going back to your roots, putting on walking boots, or just being who you are can be enough in itself, so no matter when, where or how.

Write, if that's what you want to do.

To Devils Bridge, and to High Heaven, through mist and storm, onward we shall go.

Even when it's hard to speak and your tongue tied and lose all sense of the motion, just go on, carry forth the flag and place glory where it stands. As you leave the dead behind and look to the future, the battle may be won, but the war is far from over.

For inside I have ideas, I think of these things and I write them down, whether or not they make much sense, some combine into poetry, some go onto become a novel and others just remain an idea.

Ideas

I could have a million ideas!
Over and under,
What's it all about?

Story or Play,
Song and dance
If only I had a chance!

The end my friend,
That's what I'd like.
Just one of my ideas,
Just one to be finished...

Yes an idea, my idea
To end my friend,
Just to end.

So if I'm late, it's because I'm dead, but my words go on into the night, like bats from out of hibernation, like rain from a cloud. Falling, the plot thickens, the blood dries up and the body is left cold.

They say that if you don't know me be now, then how can you ever know me at all, but then who are we really?

Inside are we just a mesh of veins, DNA, body parts, emotions, complex workings of heart and mind, simple bowl movements or structured bone, flexed muscle, reproductive parts, those used in sexual intercourse, or for women their breasts that could feed another.

Balls, boobs, bums, bogies, backs, bones, biceps, body in all.

We all look and listen and touch and feel and are human in the best form that we know. We are not alien, unless we are alien to ourselves and others.

We taste, we sample life and we go down a path that leads to one place and one place alone. It is "The Road To Death".

Only let us not be melancholy, let us smile, let us leave the inside and get on with some decent filling, let us take bread, drink wine, indulge in chocolate, bacon sandwiches and all manner of good food and drink, fill your insides until they are fit to burst, fill thy mind and body, soul to soul and souls apart take all the filling you can get.

Let us continue with the drivel and merge into the next chapter as we fill up and take stock, as we fill our lives with all that we can, filling each day in at a time.

Filling

Filing is just what we do, we are all filling to each other, there are a great and many wonderful things we can do to fill our lives, and to start I recommend reading my own books, and of course books of others, but I'd be foolish not to mention my "Run Of The Mill" series.

For "Run Of The Mill" has a little of something for everyone, it goes into music, the weather, God, oh yes, we even talk on the taboo if you will as excitement and entertainment are abundant just as is a choice of fillings for sandwiches or religion.

I'm filling in the stars, the ones that are like diamonds in the sky.

I'm filling in my life each and every second, every minute of the day and every day of the year, as years pass and I fill my life with many things, watch new shows on the television, see new films, listen to both old and new music, enjoy new friends, new experiences, perhaps even new lovers.

Do you know something I just noticed that a "minute" as in portion of time is also spelt the same as "minute" that is something small, but then a minute of time is not long at all is it, really?

So there is no more time for fooling around.

As we also note that 'Contents' is also in thesaurus terms, 'Filling' and 'Inside' as well as lastly, 'Stuffing'. So you see using a thesaurus to find a different word, but one that relates to the first word you chose, this itself is a great way to play with poetry and the English language as a whole, but you can then go onto insert the odd 'foreign' word if you like, not being disrespectful, but meaning a word from a different language.

Go and find poetry in a picture and be filled with words that will burst out onto paper.

For sometimes all we have is here and now.

As a smell sparks a memory, pizza reminds me of Rome, chocolate the streets of France or Belgium.

I'm bare foot, I tell bear faced lies, I'm caught in a bear trap and lost to the bare necessities, looking in bare windows, the satellite navigation system simply notes to "Bear left" but when you look, there isn't one there.

I painted myself into a corner once. It was a nice picture, but not what I was really aiming for...

Morning has broken, as if out of jail. I say morning has broken, it comes from that song, and if you don't know it then it does not matter, but for those of you who are now singing part of the song, going "Morning has broken, just like the..." and so on, then I apologise, for you'll now have that partly stuck in your head and it happens all the time when you hear a part of a song you know all too well, every now and then you just repeat a segment of it over and over again, for that is the part that has filled your head, you forget the rest.

You only know what you should know... (I can't live, if living is with you, I mean without you...)

I can't give anymore nonsense, but I'll try...

I guess this is just the way the story goes, in my eyes I see the words, but I don't know what I should know...

I have to laugh a moment while you're working out all the parts of the song there, while I fill another page up with mindless drivel, drivel that was best left un-typed, locked up.

Perhaps locked in a cell with morning until the headline read "Morning has broken!" and then it went on to lead you to a tale of how the once renowned jewel thief and master con-artist 'Dave Morning' had broken out of jail yesterday and was now at large.

There's a funny thing, if the 'criminal' is at 'large' then why don't the police simply go to 'large' and capture the crook?

I'm filling you up with little odd bits and stuffing as much as I can into this book, before I decide enough is enough.

So you should know the facts and beware the acts of others, I'm in a rush to get to Berlin. Fast asleep on a train inside my mind the pixies play. I see the past, I look to a bright and orange future, I ponder all I have and all that is to come and go.

As there is a new gold in the new day as sunlight strikes across the hay and the farm is filled with noise and laughter, children are playing, school is out, summer is here and winter beckons, all too soon the moon shall pass the sun and night shall occur during the day as I eclipse into memories and fade out a shady remark.

I haven't been here, but I have and I haven't...

Over the hills and far away, I fill the valley with song. I sing my melody as if nothing ever happened. The music here is hauntingly familiar, and my heart cries out, there is no doubt as to what just happened.

I need tea Rupert.

So pause and reflect, go back a page, or don't. I no longer care, for I just fill the page and continue to keep filling and filling until my life or the book is full.

I'm just throwing things in there for throwing them in sake.

I saw Red Kites flying in, they filled the sky, and I paused and pondered as I filled the path ahead with my footprints. I trekked along and forged through valley and across stream. I walked towards the sea.

And there I saw...

Two men in a boat,
The water was blue and indigo,
Along the insensible channel
They steam along.

For now we are all filled in and we have the filling chapter full, I guess it is time to turn the page, to go on and continue, to persevere in the deluge of 'Drivel' to admire the written word, to come across a single token, a moment of pure genius and a sole piece of text that will strike a chord for evermore and will always find a place in both your heart and mind.

And so I press on into the next chapter, I'm about to stuff this book just a little more. So Stuffing is all I can do for now.

Stuffing

You know the stuff, it's got sage and onion in it, some have cranberries and orange, but they all go into a dead duck, chicken or turkey if it's Christmas.

Stuffing in sandwiches is great, to just make some up, boil the kettle and then mix and spread it all out or roll it into balls and place onto a baking try, put the tray in a mid to high heated oven and wait. As the smell drifts into the kitchen and the stuffing is cooked, slice or take a ball and allow to cool slightly, before serving. If sliced place into sandwich with turkey or ham, or with cheese on toast, a welsh rabbit, but made in your own country.

Through the country and across rivers and fields, taking paths and roads, passing trees and hedge rows, heading east or west, north or south. In which direction I do not know.

My Lysander aircraft sits on a runway, I am waiting for my pilot.

I'll have the black stuff, just half a pint, and some whiskey, a glass of wine and cider for Rosie, lager for Jim.

As possession is nine tenths of the law, I can but refrain to think on what the last tenth might be, but then this stuff is all stuff and at eight fifteen I must be stuffed, I must be full and my insides content with booze.

A dragon breaths fire, even if it is a stuffed toy, I don't care what it is stuffed with, just get it away from the flames of desire.

I'm going back to Monday Morning, Tuesday on a train, Wednesday I'm back to work again then Thursday it's to see a friend and not a foe, and Friday was once a Framework day.

As for Saturday and Sunday, well who knows?

I prefer solid ale, not tepid beer, a cool drink on a summer's day is refreshing and I'm not stuffing things into my shorts.

The 'Budgie Smugglers' are here, they take the bird from the cage and go towards the border in hopes of getting across.

There it was in the paper the other day, "Two Budgie Smugglers Arrested" it went on to say that the two were caught on the Mexican/American Border, for you may not know it, but there is currently a Budgie shortage in America. Way down in Mexico you can buy a single yellow budgie for just a few Pesos, or around fifty pence, and then if you can smuggle it across into America, places up near Chicago will pay anywhere from fifty to a hundred dollars for one, or about thirty-five to eighty pounds. Just for a simple little yellow bird, a Budgie.

You cannot be too careful when you choose your enemies, not that I figure you'd want a choice in enemies. Only I'd choose a dead enemy, if I had a choice, there's last chance of the enemy coming to get you that way.

Not that there should be a chance in the first place.

It recalls to mind the time I had sambucca. All those wonderful colours, red, green and blue, but vomit is often brown and so is poo.

I don't need you, you don't need me, and I don't know what to do anymore... It's just a line, from a song that went on but I was the one. I played my drums; I struck the guitar and went far. I got to number one. So please do sing along... la-la laa Lar ...De-de da Dum...

I like my English humour, but then what of Irish or German humour? I really should leave these questions until we get to that chapter!

Basically I'm at a loose end, now that in itself is an odd thing to say, wait a moment I've got a chapter called Oddness yet to come also, so I best get on with some stuffing!

For I wish I was in the land of cotton, I'm not sure if there is a land actually called 'cotton' I think it refers to where 'cotton' grows. If I say 'look away, look away', then don't actually look away, it's just part of something, some random affect of stuffing the pages with words.

I'm to ere the breed of thistles and I shall sail out to sea. All the men are off to fish and catch the mighty whale. I deplore whale hunting! I merely mention it as a reference to Moby Dick.

I've got Murphy's luck, so I best give it him back.

Perhaps a jaunt into the country, along some cycle highway, a bridge too far and a journey back along the dusty road.

Cycling gives you time to stop and admire the view or stop and rest and enjoy a pint or two.

I think of liquor, the rum, the vodka, the ebb of brandy, the dram of whiskey a tipple of sherry and a splash of vermouth and martini. Take tequila back and see my rum shine as wine and women make merry with song.

Along the twisted and flowing river, the barge found its way.

It stopped at a jetty and I walked from water to land.

Land scared by man, man who needed power.

Power for mindless television, endless records and street lights, those Christmas decorations and all manner of machines that make things, such as toast or tea, machines that wash clothes and a machine to write a book upon.

From one machine to another, from cooling towers of concrete to pylons of steel that cross the green and fertile land. The dusty black coal burns to give man his endless power.

Somewhere in the distance there are Ogres.

The worker
The tackle of words
The punt along a stream
The safety man arrives
The inexpressible poem is read
The ship sails
The life is gone
The stuffing knocked out
The place ablaze
The misty eyes,
The beating heart
The rise and fall
The emotion, the potion
The time
The poem
The next few lines

In any place, in any time
At some moment,
Between here and now...

I lost something, and yet
I found happiness, but got lonely.
Lonely without you,
Alone in the dark, looking for a spark...

Here we both are,
Lost and lonely
In a wild landscape

But together we are one,
So let us go over the hills and far away

Let us escape this moment
To go and make love

Or if you'd prefer to pause for a nice cup of tea
instead, don't let me stop you, for I have just finished
one, cup of tea that is, before you think anything else.

After all there was Ike and me and there was time for
one last cup of tea. For D-Day and the War and for the
death of Hitler and Stalin, the remorse at the loss of
Churchill and the pain in losing a Queen, we gain
something and stuff ourselves into the realms of
fantasy. I see the dawn of early day, I pause and
reflect, I stuff it all back into a place, somewhere I can
easily find it all. One day it becomes a film.

Films:

I love a good film, on a sunny day in the height of summer, all wrapped up and cosy, with a mug of hot chocolate and some popcorn, nothing quite beats the home cinema. I say 'summer' but of course mean 'winter' the actual winter, the one that happens from around December to February, as those are the winter months. March, April and May is spring. June, July and August is summer and September, October and November make up autumn.

Only it's not always the case, but I like the way I put it, three months to each season, dividing the year quite nicely and making winter occur twice every year, as we start off in January, with winter, and not with spring.

Why does the New Year not start in spring?

Never mind back to films and "Groundhog Day" starring Bill Murray, it's a great film in which he lives the same day over and over again, giving you the idea that if you could just keep having the same moment over and over again, repeat time as it were, knowing what was to come, then what would you do in that situation?

There's a scene that is a moment off odd humour in itself that I only came across recently.

Bill is staying at a local bed and breakfast.

He wakes yet again on the same day, its Ground Hog Day all over again.

Bill comes down from his room in his pyjamas for breakfast, he asks "Mrs Lancaster" the owner of the bed and breakfast if she has ever had "Déjà vu" and she replies, "I don't know, but I can ask in the kitchen."

The implication is that déjà vu is a food or breakfast item, perhaps some sort of French dish?

I actually thought that déjà vu was spelt as three different things, as in "da ja vu" so silly me there. Perhaps it was the fault of a certain television channel?

If you ever come across the words "da ja vu" in one of my books and I've not put déjà vu, then perhaps it's best not to tell me, after all I am human, well I think I am...

Now during the film Labyrinth, when David Bowie sings the song "Magic Dance" and he says, "You remind me of the babe." And the goblins reply, "Who do?" Bowie says, "You Do?" Goblins reply "Do what?" It's the whole, who do, you do, do what, bit that I find great. For when you think upon it. The lyrics flow, it's only short, but for a moment, if you get stuck on it so that it's: -

"Who do?" then a pause, followed by "You do!" and a slight pause before, "Do what?".

For 'do what' in itself is a non direct, but affirmed question that has no relative meaning, but a direct point, as to refer "Do What?" is not in pretext, it should be more along the line of, "What do you do?"

You can ignore all the questions back there, but please enjoy the films if you've not seen them before.

Have you ever seen one of those films, either a western or a war film and someone shouts, "Fire at Will!", well what get's me, is why is it always Will, and not some other poor chap, and come to think of it, all the enemy, or the persons to whom you are about to fire at, well they have to do is say, "We're not Will', only of course I'm being daft, but then this whole book has been daft.

For what "Fire at Will" actually means is that you can fire your weapon as you please, shoot as many of the enemy as you can before they shoot you...

Films are great and for me there is none other than a good 'Bond' film, it was Moonraker, the very first James Bond film I saw, igniting an everlasting fascination with all things Bond, from then on in I was hooked. It was the overture, the song "Moonraker" sung by Shirley Bassey, making it her third and final James Bond Theme.

It's the run up to Bond going into space, another encounter with 'Jaws', the chase in Venice.

Moonraker to me is key in a series of well thought out films and also it's a great song, amongst those before and the ones that were yet to come, when Tina Turner sang 'Goldeneye' it was amongst my favourites.

I enjoy all the Bond films and I look forward to the next one, I dread to think that they might one day stop, but then all good things come to an end, don't they?

Just as I started to live and let die, the man with the golden came in. I paused and we looked at each other, it was for your eyes only that I showed you how diamonds are forever and how the goldeneye set out in search of the moonraker. So I live to die another day, but what of my gold finger and when I sent you flowers from Russia with love? Looking back with a view to a kill as the thunderball rolls, and the lottery of life and death is eluded by Dr. No and the time is now, take your licence to kill and leave, go back to the living daylights and forget that you only live twice. I'm no longer here on her majesty's secret service, instead I come when tomorrow never dies and the spy who loved me is lost in Casino Royale. And so the world is not enough, but for the octopussy it is a game, it is like skyfall and the dark, I can only say never. Only I must never say never again and the quantum of solace is for us all. It is a spectre, all the colours combined, but none are more bright or dark than the colour of Bond.

Did you spot a James Bond film title in there, including the very last time in which the great Sean Connery plays the title role, Edward Fox plays 'M' in a re-working of the film "Thunderball". "Never Say Never Again" features of all people Rowan Atkinson, who is better known as 'Mr. Bean' and there is a thought itself, if James Bond were to meet Mr. Bean...

There's an odd thing itself a remake or rehash of a previous film, but with slightly different plot or setting. Often more than not what happens is the first few films come out and then a prequel turns up.

Do you get frustrated that after the first film the prequel comes out, where is the sequel? But then are there films that have too many sequels?

As sometimes you get to a point and think, have they made one film too many? And you could argue this for James Bond, but to me it's a different film each time in a series featuring a main character, James Bond and the villains he encounters as part of his role On Her Majesty's Secret Service.

Some sequels are great and well thought of, for instance the so called trilogies where you get three great films that all tie in nicely together, 'Die Hard' was one of these great trilogies before a fourth and fifth appeared. Only they themselves both the fourth and fifth 'Die Hard' films aren't all that bad.

I guess the best three films to watch back to back that come to my mind is "The Matrix" set.

But enough of this and that, instead let's go from 'The Great Escape' to 'Grease'.

There are moments in a film we can all relate to, be it 'Back To The Future' another good trilogy, 'Last Of The Mohicans', if your 'Footloose' or enjoying a classic animated film by 'Disney' or 'Dream Works' it might be time for a shoot out and explosions like those found in films like 'The Good, The Bad And The Ugly' or 'Kelly's Heroes' that also has an element of comedy in it.

To laugh with or at films is good, when they make you cry or think, they make you jump and scream or run for cover, they excite and enthral, they inspire us as they weave their tale onto the screen.

Films are films, it's always good to enjoy one at home or at the cinema, and a trip to the cinema to see a new film, well that has to top it all. Getting ready going out, the tickets, the crowd of other people who are all keen to see the new film, or perhaps the sequel to the first, they are waiting to see what happens next, they are caught in the story, just as you are caught in this 'Drivel' and this book.

It's the film we all enjoy, we might have only one, or maybe more. It's oddness next and that's all.

Oddness

At first I thought there was nothing,
At first we heard the jingling of her keys.

No words are spoken, it just my hand reaching in the darkness, and if the light goes out, we've had it.

Some, not all, like the smell of their own farts. I'm not one of them, for I try not to fart, but then we all need to release wind, some do so by farting, others by talking, namely Politicians.

> On a Christmas tree,
> There are Christmas lights,
> It's Christmas time...
> Soon we'll all be opening
> Christmas Presents...

If you want to write a poem, you can actually start with just one word. That's all you need, take Christmas for example. Now make a list of every word that can follow Christmas, for example:-

Christmas lights, Christmas tree, Christmas presents, Christmas time, Christmas pudding, Christmas joy, Christmas decorations, Christmas cards and so on...

There in itself is the making of a poem, try a name.

Ed's book, Ed's 'Drivel', Ed's life, Ed's look, Ed's feel

Or try something like, "It's", so that you go along the same way, for example.

It's great, it's a poem, it's a boy, it's party time, it's all in a name, it's life, it's a start, it's a school, it's a word, it's a day, it's a year, it's a new experience, it's a girlfriend, it's a moment, it's this, it's that, it's all over, it's death.

Use a feeling perhaps, like Happy, or Sad. And use the two together, find the opposite, so you get something and again for example:-

Happy day, sad day, happy night, sad night, happy time, sad time and so on or so forth.

Think about a shadow, so you get a 'Shadow of doubt' or a 'Shadow of evil' or even a 'Shadow of gold'?

Last night the fair was in town, the sound of music, the merry-go-round.

The cold light of day
The cold black of night

Into the blue, out of the blue

Away from the blue

With my hungry eyes and my hungry heart, I hope that we shall never depart. Farewell oddness.

Questions?

Everyone has questions, but do they have the answers?

Is not the idea of a question, more of not having an answer to everything, but to most things. For example we all know that the question of adding two and two together, well two plus two no doubt makes four. Only to the more complex question of "Are we alone in the Universe?" One could argue yes and no at the same time, as when you ask "Are 'we' alone?". Who is we and what would you mean by 'alone', so the question itself only adds more questions to it...

In this way I ask you to ask me any question, it does not matter if there is an answer or if there isn't one at all, it's just that you can have some good fun with a question. For who is this book for?

What is love?

Who did what, with how and when?

There's a joke about "Who's on first" in which you refer to a person and not the question. It's a baseball thing, as 'first' refers to 'base' or the position on the playing ground.

Only let us get back to some more 'Questions'...

What have you done?

What's in a word?

What's in a name?

Now is there a sense of sarcasm in that, for the way in which you read it, might be different to the way in which not only can you say it, but also the way I wrote it.

Read back "What have you done?" and put the emphasis on 'you', and you'll imply that there is only one person responsible, if you emphasise the 'done' then it is more of wanting to know just what you have 'done', for it might turn out to be a good thing.

I also have to question not only how does this read, but how does it sound? For how do you sound English, or Welsh, or Scottish, French, German, Dutch or Icelandic? Do they have regional accents like in Yorkshire, Norfolk, Essex, in Newcastle and Ireland? Is Russian different in Moscow than it is in Siberia?

Are the Japanese talking in accents different than in the north compared to the south, for the United States of America has a trend of accents. In New York the accent is different to that of a Texan, or even a Mexican.

Is alien a language that we do know, but can't say? Is Norwegian really Swedish, but with Finish tones and a Danish trend that can be found as far away as Egypt?

I mean 'Finish' as in "Finish" the language, as from Finland, I don't think I have correct spelling, but then this is mere drivel, it does not have to have the correct spelling half the time, just as long as it gets to some point and a message across, just long as I continue to rabble to 'tosh' (toss) out the rubbish, throw back nonsense and recline in poppycock as I adore words in all the idiocy they have, I battle with claptrap and rot and come to terms with drivel and foolishness.

So to more questions and questions followed by questions, but don't feel you have to find an answer, try not to look too hard for the answer, for one might spend a whole life just looking for an answer to just one question.

What is black, but cannot be seen?

Is blood red?

Is blood thicker than water?

And when I say 'thicker' I don't imply some sort of knowledge, as if water and blood had some form of intelligence. But then they must have some form of knowing, not in a human sense, well blood might, for blood carries all the oxygen and nutrients around the body, and water regenerates the body, but it flows, it is taken by gravity or the lay of the land, water comes from clouds, it lies in big lakes and forms small seas and large oceans.

So both water and blood are good and must have some form of intellect to be able to do the job in which we imply upon them.

It's a bit like saying "As thick as two short planks", as two short planks have no knowledge or brains for that matter at all, in fact what would two short planks be good for?

Who is simple, as its one or more people.
What, well something happened...
When, we want to know the time, or the place...
How, it's the explanation of what and when, it is then perhaps we ask, 'Why?'

'Why?'. Is a very great question, for just asking it alone, one might never get an answer.

Why is this not a book of poetry?

Where is the moonlight trail that leads to your side?

Where is Edward when you need him?

Who's Harry?

How much love is a box of chocolates, or a bunch of flowers worth?

Do you have a second-hand emotion? Suggesting that you no longer have a brand new emotion, but merely one that has already been used.

Where would the birds go, if there was no winter?

Is the night all a dream? As if you are unconscious in sleep, then how do you know you dream at all?

Does my heart beat to the rhythm of a drum?

How many tigers are there in Britain? Forty-two, was my first guess, but if each zoo has at least one and there are, hang on, how many zoos are there? Not to mention a place near Lincoln that had tigers...

Has it got a zoo? Lincoln that is, and not London or Newcastle.

Where does it all begin?

Is everyone and everything on Facebook?

In the daylight, do you hide?

Can I go on to ask more questions?

Remember those maths questions like: 'If Mary has two oranges, and Ralph has an orange and a tomato, Lewis has a banana and May-ling has a pear and an orange. How many pieces of fruit are there altogether?

Who is Mary and Ralph, or May-ling for that matter?

And the tomato, who brings a whole tomato to school for lunch, I can understand if the tomato were sliced and in a sandwich, but a whole one?

I've had forms to fill in that ask about sexuality and it always gets me that "Prefer not to say" is an option, as for humour one could propose that itself, "Prefer not to say" is a sexuality! I'm no longer heterosexual, lesbians and homosexuals are shifting, the bi-sexual trend is gone and now we are all "Prefer not to say"...

The last census would have been a bit dull if everyone had put "Prefer not to say".

Were you dancing in the rain last night? I thought it was you?

Do you know where this train goes, once it leaves the station?

Who counts the money, underneath the bar?

Which yellow bird fills its nest with lemons?

You say my charmer, to that we can swear, where are the words we so long for in the dead of night?

What's become of you?

How do you make a rhyme? Do the Crime?

Does it matter, where we die?

Where are the doubts, when you need them?

Why do you write?

Is this reality? Asked the man as he got off the bus, or train or even out of a taxi?

Are we all alone to begin with?

There's a stack of wooden pallets over there, pallet on top of pallet, do they complain?

A language I overheard in conversation, it sounds as if I've heard it before. Is that French? That is to say, it's not French is it?

Are you from a film?

'Got a light?' I don't smoke, but I did have a torch on me for my bicycle...

Is the sun coming to thaw the frost?

At first I saw the frosted leaves on the ground. I thought where is the tree that the leaves have come from? Was there something I missed, or did I see the yellow and brown, if I'm blinded by the sun then perhaps I should take one leaf, for there are more to come.

I was asked a question at a writers group once. "If a plane crashes on the border of two countries, where do they bury the survivors?" At first you start to think of it, but then you realise, you don't bury 'survivors' do you.

A photograph only captures so much, does it not?

I could say that the question is meaningless, and it is in some small way, for that is all they are questions. Some to which we have an answer, and some to which we'll perhaps never have an answer.

I hope that answers your question and I'm sure you had one that was very thought provoking and one that would take time to work out and understand, and that question is not, 'Why am I reading this book?' but it's the one about life and death.

You know the one, the great question, it features in the film 'A Hitchhikers Guide To The Galaxy.'

"What is the meaning of life?"

The End

I don't know the meaning of life, it's in a dictionary.

And if you always remember that 'Sympathy is between Shit and Syphilis in the dictionary', so there is no need to thank me, but instead reflect upon a wooden box a moment, for it is just a box.

As a plane lands and the off loading begins. Here at Kabul in high heat, under the glare of sun box upon box appears, pallets laden with goods of all kinds. Wooden crates flow like a river, as far as the eye can see.

You take one, just a box. A label reads "Caution". Foodstuffs? Alcohol, that sweet nectar or just tea bags? Rations or explosives, bullets or bombs? Kevlar vests and helmets, no flowers or petticoats, no red or multi-coloured paint, just khaki and standard army green and camouflage nets.

Perhaps it's the mail, or a hundred more coffin nails. Perhaps the personnel affects of the Major, or top brass. You grab a crow bar to prise open the lid and look inside.

No weapons, no guns and glory, just the same old story, toilet rolls.

And so back you go to fizzy pop, tampax, medical supplies and the wooden crates continue till night.

It's all Sy-philosophy, which it is to say Silly (Sy) and not Syphilis-Philosophy...

The pessimistic eye of Schopenhauer's attitude to the human nature is an instance of the general pessimism of this philosophy.

You need rain to make a rainbow, and the sun, I think.

What forbids a wit to speak the truth?
Has reality become uncouth?
Who grasps the shells and the kernels?

Half a dozen more lines or so and we're done, half-cocked I shall not go off, for half-way through this book I hoped you'd carry on and not leave it behind.

Don't get half lost, get half drunk, don't be lost and lonely, try to enjoy life as much as you can.

Yesterday is gone, tomorrow is yet to come and today is a gift, that's why we call it 'The PRESENT'

Thank you and farewell, I now recognize and allow time to say goodbye. It's been great writing this, even if it is only 'Drivel' but then I concede it's actually really good in parts. Take care.

Acknowledgements

Firstly a huge thank you to you the dear reader for putting up with this book, well done! I'd also like to thank my mum, Lincoln Creative Writers, A Word In Edgeways, my nephews Liam, Charlie and Elliott and my Niece Sacha, aka Little Kimberley, that is My sister, Sacha's mum, Kimberley. Not Kimberley the place in South Africa.

A great thanks to my once neighbour Dawn, to Boultham Library and Lincolnshire Health Support Service, to whom I used to work for, just Lincolnshire Health Support Service and not the others.

Thank you to the RSPB, for all their wonderful reserves, projects, all the people, especially the volunteers and the abundance of Nature...

I'd like to thank the Pope, God if there was one, and the two Aliens who abducted me last night, but did not use a probe, the mean things...

Lastly then don't fling this useless book away, give it to someone for Christmas, they'll love you for the rest of your life...

All the best,

E. Chandler

Ed Chandler.

15326559R00031

Printed in Great Britain
by Amazon